GALE
CENGAGE Learning·

Novels for Students, Volume 14

Staff

Editor: Jennifer Smith.

Contributing Editors: Anne Marie Hacht, Michael L. LaBlanc, Ira Mark Milne, Daniel Toronto, Carol Ullmann.

Managing Editor, Content: Dwayne D. Hayes.

Managing Editor, Product: David Galens.

Publisher, Literature Product: Mark Scott.

Literature Content Capture: Joyce Nakamura, *Managing Editor*. Sara Constantakis, *Editor*.

Research: Victoria B. Cariappa, *Research Manager*. Sarah Genik, Ron Morelli, Tamara Nott, Tracie A. Richardson, *Research Associates*. Nicodemus Ford, *Research Assistant*.

Permissions: Maria L. Franklin, *Permissions Manager*. Shalice Shah-Caldwell, *Permissions*

Associate. Deborah Freitas, *IC Coordinator/Permissions Associate.*

Manufacturing: Mary Beth Trimper, *Manager, Composition and Electronic Prepress.* Evi Seoud, *Assistant Manager, Composition Purchasing and Electronic Prepress.* Stacy Melson, *Buyer.*

Imaging and Multimedia Content Team: Barbara Yarrow, *Manager.* Randy Bassett, *Imaging Supervisor.* Robert Duncan, Dan Newell, Luke Rademacher, *Imaging Specialists.* Pamela A. Reed, *Imaging Coordinator.* Leitha Etheridge-Sims, Mary Grimes, David G. Oblender, *Image Catalogers.* Robyn V. Young, *Project Manager.* Dean Dauphinais, *Senior Image Editor.* Kelly A. Quin, *Image Editor.*

Product Design Team: Pamela A. E. Galbreath, *Senior Art Director.* Michael Logusz, *Graphic Artist.*

agency, institution, publication, service, or individual does not imply endorsement of the editors or publisher. Errors brought to the attention of the publisher and verified to the satisfaction of the publisher will be corrected in future editions.

This publication is a creative work fully protected by all applicable copyright laws, as well as by misappropriation, trade secret, unfair competition, and other applicable laws. The authors and editors of this work have added value to the underlying factual material herein through one or more of the following: unique and original selection, coordination, expression, arrangement, and classification of the information. All rights to this publication will be vigorously defended.

Sula

Toni Morrison

1973

Introduction

Sula, published in 1973 in New York, is Toni Morrison's second novel. Set in the early 1900s in a small Ohio town called Medallion, it tells the story of two African-American friends, Sula and Nel, from their childhood through their adulthood and Sula's death. Morrison drew on her own small-town, Midwestern childhood to create this tale of conformity and rebellion.

Morrison began writing *Sula* in 1969, a time of great activism among African Americans and others who were working toward equal civil rights and opportunities. The book addresses issues of racism, bigotry, and suppression of African Americans; it depicts the despair people feel when they can't get decent jobs, and the determination of some to survive. Eva, for example, cuts off her leg in order to get money to raise her family. Morrison shows how, faced with racist situations, some people had to grovel to whites simply to get by, as Helene does on a train heading through the South. Others, however, fought back, as Sula does when she threatens some white boys who are harassing her and Nel.

The novel was well received by critics, who particularly praised her vivid imagery, strong characterization, and poetic prose, as well as her terse, realistic dialogue. The book was nominated for a National Book Award in 1974

Author Biography

Nobel laureate Toni Morrison was born Chloe Anthony Wofford on February 18, 1931, in Lorain, Ohio. She was the second of four children of Ramah and George Wofford. She studied English at Howard University, and earned a master's degree in English literature from Cornell, where she wrote her thesis on William Faulkner. She then became a teacher of English at Texas Southern University, and later at Howard University, where she worked until 1964.

While teaching at Howard, Morrison began to write. She told an interviewer for Borders that her beginning was almost accidental; she joined a group of colleagues at Howard University who had formed a writer's group and because members couldn't come unless they had written something, she began writing a short story, which eventually became her first novel.

In 1958 the author married Harold Morrison, an architect, with whom she had two sons, but in 1964 they divorced. After the divorce, Morrison moved to Syracuse, New York, where she supported her family by working as a book editor at Random House. During her tenure there, she edited the work of many well-known African-American authors, including Toni Cade Bambara, Gayl Jones, and Angela Davis.

Her first book, *The Bluest Eye*, was completed

in the mid-1960s, but Morrison received many rejections of the novel until 1969, when it was finally accepted by Holt, Rinehart, and Winston, and published in 1970. Like all of Morrison's work, it considers issues of race and the African-American experience. *Sula* was published in 1973 and was nominated for a National Book Award in 1974. *Song of Solomon* was published in 1977 and won the National Book Critics Circle Award for that year. *Tar Baby* was published in 1981, and made best-seller lists for four months. *Beloved* (1987), which tells the story of ex-slaves haunted by their past, was widely acclaimed, as was *Jazz* (1992).

In 1993, Morrison was awarded the Nobel Prize for literature, and thus became the first African American and only the eighth woman ever to win the award. According to Maureen O'Brien in *Publishers Weekly*, Morrison said, "What is most wonderful for me personally is to know that the Prize has at last been awarded to an African American. I thank God that my mother is alive to see this day." In 1996, she received the National Book Foundation Medal for Distinguished Contribution to American Letters.

Paradise, set in an all-black town in Oklahoma, was published in 1998. Morrison has also written and edited many works of literary criticism, as well as a play, *Dreaming Emmett*. Her essays and interviews have been widely published in both popular and scholarly periodicals.

Since 1988, Morrison has been a professor at Princeton University, where she holds the Robert F.

Goheen Professorship of the Humanities and is the chair of the Creative Writing Program. According to an article on the Web site *Voices from the Gaps*, Morrison was giving a lecture at Princeton when a student asked her who she wrote for. Morrison said,

> I want to write for people like me, which is to say black people, curious people, demanding people—people who can't be faked, people who don't need to be patronized, people who have very, very high criteria.

Introduction

Sula opens with a description of "The Bottom," the African-American section of a town called Medallion in Ohio, which has been bought by whites, who force out the remaining inhabitants and level the old buildings to create a golf course. The Bottom got its name from a joke played on a slave by a white farmer, who said he would give the slave his freedom, and a section of rich bottom land, in exchange for doing some difficult chores. The slave fulfilled his work and the farmer gave him his freedom, but was reluctant to give away fertile bottom land. Instead, he told the slave that a section of eroded land high in the hills was really bottom land, because from God's point of view, it was "the bottom of heaven." The slave, not knowing any better, accepted the land, which turned out to be worthless for farming, and thus the African-American settlement was founded. The Bottom subsequently has a rich history as a lively African-American community.

1919

Shadrack is a shell-shocked veteran of World War I who is returned to the Bottom by a sheriff who figures out that he was originally from there. He lives in a shack and becomes famous for his invented holiday, National Suicide Day, which he celebrates on January 3rd of each year, starting in 1920. On this holiday, people who don't want to continue living with the fear of death are invited to kill themselves, thus taking control of a normally uncontrollable event. Although this holiday initially frightens people in the Bottom, eventually they become used to it and it becomes a part of local culture.

1920

Helene, Nel's mother, is the daughter of a prostitute, but was raised by her grandmother in a strict and sheltered environment. Helene marries Wiley Wright and moves to Medallion, where she lives an upright and respectable life, and forces Nel to do the same. When she receives a letter saying her grandmother, Cecile, is very ill, she reluctantly decides to go to New Orleans to see her. Her reluctance comes from the widespread racism in the South, and on the train ride to New Orleans, her fears are realized. The African-American passengers must sit in segregated cars, and there are no bathrooms for them; they have to use fields near the train tracks. Helene also must grovel to a white train conductor who is harassing her.

Cecile dies before Helene's arrival, but Helene sees her mother, Rochelle, and introduces Nel to her. Nel is fascinated and shocked by her grandmother's exotic looks and behavior. All of these experiences change Nel; after the trip, for the first time, she realizes that she is a separate person, an individual. She meets another girl, Sula, who comes from a wild family but appears at first to be calm and quiet. Helene, swayed by this good behavior, allows Nel to be friends with Sula, and the friendship grows.

1921

This chapter describes Sula's family, particularly her grandmother Eva. When Eva and her three children are abandoned by her husband, she goes away, then returns eighteen months later with only one leg and ten thousand dollars. Rumors say that she cut off her leg in order to collect the insurance money. She builds a huge, rambling house, where she lives on the top floor and gets around in a wheelchair. She uses the rest of the space to house "her children, friends, strays, and a constant stream of boarders."

Eva's daughter, Pearl, marries and moves away; her daughter, Hannah, is a promiscuous widow, and she and her daughter, Sula, live in Eva's house; and a third child, Plum, fights in World War I and returns home a drug addict. When Eva finds out the extent of his addiction, she pours kerosene on him and burns him to death while he's in a drug-induced, euphoric haze.

Media Adaptations

- *Sula* (1997) is an unabridged audio book narrated by Morrison and available through Random House.

1922

Sula and Nel are now twelve years old, and are just becoming interested in men. They are best friends, and have a deep understanding, despite their different personalities. Nel is calm and reliable, while Sula is unpredictable and even violent. When they're harassed by some white boys, Sula cuts off the tip of her own finger to show them how tough she is, which scares them away.

Sula overhears her mother telling some friends that she loves Sula, but doesn't like her. Sula is deeply hurt, but says nothing. She and Nel go down to the river, seeking shade from the heat, and see Chicken Little, a little boy. They play with him, and Sula grabs his arms and swings him around; her grip slips, and he flies out into the river and drowns. Frightened, Sula runs to see if Shadrack—who is in the nearest dwelling—has seen the incident. Shadrack doesn't even give Sula a chance to ask her question, instead saying, "Always," which Sula takes as a threat. Terrified, she flees, and Nel tells her it's not her fault, it was just an accident. Neither of them confesses to the killing or goes for any more help.

Chicken Little's body is found by a white man, who fishes it out and is annoyed at the inconvenience of dealing with a dead black child. Three days later, Chicken Little's remains are returned to his mother, and his funeral is held. Nel and Sula both attend, but they say nothing.

1923

The Bottom is in the middle of a summer drought, and Hannah asks Eva if she ever loved her children. Eva is angered by this question, and says that the sacrifice of her leg to keep them alive proves that she loves them. Hannah asks why, if she loved her children, she burned Plum to death. Eva says that she had many hard times keeping Plum alive as a child, that the war and the addiction had turned him back into a child, and that this time, she didn't have the power to save him. She says she killed him out of love, wanting him to die as a man.

She explains that she held Plum lovingly in her arms before she killed him.

Hannah tells Eva that she dreamed of a red wedding dress, an omen of violence. She also tells her that Sula has been acting up lately, which everybody assumes is because she is getting her period. Sula is not the only person in the Bottom who is acting strangely. The heat and the drought have everyone on edge. Eva's comb is missing, and the shape and color of Sula's birthmark seem to be changing.

Like everyone else in the Bottom, Hannah begins doing the summer canning of fruits and vegetables. When she goes out in the yard and lights the canning fire, her dress catches fire and bursts into flame. Eva hurls herself out of her wheelchair and through the second-story window, hoping she can drag herself across the yard fast enough to save Hannah, but Hannah runs out of the yard and becomes severely burned when neighbors try to put out the fire. An ambulance arrives, but Hannah dies on the way to the hospital. Eva, who was injured in the fall, almost bleeds to death.

While she is in the hospital recovering, Eva remembers the dream of the red wedding dress and realizes the fire is the event it foretold. She also realizes that during the fire, Sula was on the porch, watching her own mother burn to death and doing nothing to help. She tells her friends about this, but they all say Sula was probably so shocked that she couldn't do anything to help. Eva, however, believes that Sula intentionally let her mother die.

1927

Four years have passed, and Nel begins a relationship with Jude Greene, a waiter who wants to get a job on a road-building crew. His dream comes to nothing, however, because the road crew will not hire African Americans even if, like Jude, they are better-equipped for the hard labor than the "thin-armed white boys." This makes Jude bitter, and he asks Nel to marry him, hoping marriage will make him feel more manly. Nel happily accepts. Helene, Nel's mother, is excited, too, and plans a big, extravagant wedding unlike any ever held in the Bottom before.

The wedding is a fine event, and Nel is her usual traditional, proper self, looking forward to a settled life as a good wife. After the wedding, she notices Sula slip away. Sula leaves town, and does not return for almost ten years.

1937

Sula comes back to the Bottom, wearing expensive clothes, on the same day that a huge flock of robins arrives. The townspeople link these two events, considering them both evil omens. Sula walks through streets full of bird excrement as the people stare at her. She finally gets to Eva's house, and the first thing Eva says is, "I might have knowed them birds meant something."

Their relationship is now cold. Eva tells Sula that she needs to find a man and settle down, but

Sula responds that she only needs herself. Sula reminds Eva that she killed Plum, and Eva reminds Sula that she stood by and watched her mother die. Sula threatens to set Eva on fire while she's sleeping, and Eva locks her out of her room. Later, Sula obtains guardianship over Eva and commits her to a shabby nursing home, shocking everyone in town.

Nel, on the other hand, is excited about Sula's return and hopes that they can rekindle their friendship; unlike everyone else, she believes that good will result from Sula's coming home. They do revive their friendship, and Nel discovers that Sula has traveled and has been to college. Sula tells Nell about her decision to put Eva in the nursing home, then asks for Nel's help, because Sula is not good at making big decisions like this.

Nel's husband Jude is interested in Sula, and she in him; one day, Nel finds them in bed together. Jude, ashamed, leaves Nel, destroying her safe little world; she has lost her husband and her best friend in the same day. She thinks of Chicken Little's funeral and how everyone released their grief in mourning for him, but she is not able to find that kind of release for her grief over the loss of her husband.

1939

Sula ends her relationship with Jude, and he moves to Detroit and never comes back. The townspeople are shocked at Sula's behavior and—

after a rumor goes around that Sula has slept with white men, "the unforgivable thing"—they decide that she's nothing but evil and trouble, and ostracize her. She becomes the scapegoat of the town, blamed for every bad thing that happens, including accidents and deaths. Despite this, or because of it, she also has a paradoxical good effect on the town; women comfort their husbands, who have been cast off from Sula after she sleeps with them, and take better care of their aging parents and grandparents, because they don't want to mirror Sula's treatment of Eva.

Sula begins seeing a man named Albert Jacks, or Ajax, who delivers milk to her house. He believes she's not interested in commitment, and neither is he; from his point of view, the relationship is only sexual. However, she begins to love him, and when he finds out, he decides to end the relationship. She is heartbroken and miserable.

1940

Three years later, Nel and Sula are still avoiding each other, but when Nel hears that Sula is sick, she visits her. Nervously, she practices what she wants to say, but Sula only wants action, not words: she directs Nel to get her some medicine. When she returns, they have a combative conversation in which Nel is annoyed by what she sees as Sula's arrogance about life. Nel accuses her of simply not dealing with her own loneliness, but Sula retorts that at least it's loneliness that she has chosen, not loneliness that has been forced on her by someone else leaving her (as Jude left Nel).

Nel becomes angry, but asks Sula why she had an affair with Jude. Sula says that she didn't love Jude, he simply filled a space in her life. Nel is shocked by this, and asks Sula if she ever thought about how it would hurt Nel. Sula tells Nel that she doesn't think sleeping with Jude should have broken up their friendship. Nel leaves, but not before Sula asks Nel how she knows she's the good one and Sula's the bad one; Sula says it could be the other way around.

Sula reflects on her life, and decides that it was a sad, worthless, and meaningless one. As she reflects, she realizes that she is not breathing and that her heart has stopped. She is dead, and didn't even feel her death. "Wait'll I tell Nel," she thinks.

1941

The townspeople are thrilled that Sula is dead, and believe that good omens indicate that more good changes are coming. The road contractors, getting ready to work on a tunnel, have announced they will hire African Americans, and a new nursing home is being built. However, all these signs come to nothing when a frigid spell keeps people inside, sickness increases, and the tunnel contractors don't hire many people after all. And without the threat of Sula as a catalyst, the townspeople turn to their old ways. Spouses are ignored, old people are neglected and children are beaten.

On January 3, Shadrack heads out for his annual celebration of Suicide Day. He thinks of Sula, the little girl who once came into his shack, the only visitor of his life, who is now dead. He is not really interested in running the Suicide Day celebration, but sets out anyway, ringing his bell. The townspeople are so demoralized by the recent hard times that many of them actually join him in the parade, needing an escape, and the procession eventually includes almost everyone in town. They turn toward the white part of town, toward the tunnel, "the place where their hope had lain since 1927." The mob begins smashing things, destroying the new construction. The tunnel collapses and great numbers of people are killed. Shadrack stands on a hill above, ringing his bell and watching the tragic event.

1965

Over twenty years later, Nel is fifty-five years old. She has spent her life taking care of her children, who are now grown, and who have forgotten her. She is alone, and the community of the Bottom has fallen apart; neighbors no longer take care of each other.

Nel, who still disapproves of Sula's putting Eva in the nursing home, visits Eva and finds her very confused. Eva talks about Chicken Little's death and accuses Nel of taking part in it. Nel tries to convince Eva that Sula, not Nel, caused his death, but Eva says, "What's the difference?" She understands that

Nel was there, and that she and Sula were so close that they were like a single person, so the guilt cannot be separated and portioned out.

Nel leaves, feeling frightened, thinking about the difference between "seeing" something and "watching" it. She saw the accident; she did not watch it. Watching implies some sort of implicit participation, some sort of acquiescence. She remembers how upset and miserable Sula was after the accident, while she, Nel, was calm. She thinks about Eva and how she used to think the old woman was so wonderful; now, she thinks, Eva was spiteful, and remembers that she didn't even go to Sula's funeral. Nel thinks about this spite, which has infected the entire town. She thinks back to the funeral, where she was the only African American in attendance. As she walks away from the gravesite, she senses something that makes her think of Sula, and realizes that she misses Sula deeply, and that when she thought she was missing her husband Jude after he left, she was really missing Sula. With this realization, she finally releases the grief that she has held pent up inside her for years.

Characters

BoyBoy

BoyBoy is Eva Peace's husband, who gives her three children, Hannah, Eva (called Pearl), and Ralph (who is called Plum), then disappears. During the time they are together, he is largely preoccupied with other women and drinking, and is rarely home. When he leaves, Eva has "$1.65, five eggs, three beets and no idea of what or how to feel." He returns three years later with a new woman, apparently having heard of Eva's new wealth and seemingly hoping for a handout, but Eva doesn't give him anything, and he disappears again.

Chicken Little

Chicken Little is a small boy who comes to play with Sula and Nel at the river. Sula picks him up and swings him around, and accidentally throws him in the river, where he drowns. His body is found downstream by a white man, who is annoyed at having to deal with it, and after the bargeman, the sheriff, and a ferryman bicker over whose responsibility it is to return to the body to the child's family, it is finally taken to the embalmer four days later.

The Deweys

The Deweys are three little boys whom Eva takes in. Regardless of their original names, she calls them all "Dewey," last name "King," and they're collectively known as "The deweys." Although they look different from each other and come from different families, their individuality is gradually subsumed in their collective identity as "deweys," to the point where they never really grow up, and Morrison writes, "The deweys remained a mystery not only during all of their lives in Medallion but after as well."

Albert Jacks

A. Jacks, or "Ajax" as he's known to everyone, is "a twenty-one-year-old pool haunt of sinister beauty." He is a favorite among women and an accomplished swearer and curser. He advises Jude about women, "All they want, man, is they own misery. Ax them to die for you and they yours for life." Later, when he's thirty-eight and Sula is twenty-nine, they become lovers. She falls in love with him, but Ajax, feeling trapped, leaves her.

Eva Peace

Although Eva is Sula's grandmother, she outlives her granddaughter, and is present during all the events of the novel. She leaves her mark on Sula, helping to shape her character.

Eva is abandoned by her husband while she is still a young mother, and, faced with the problem of supporting her family without resorting to charity, she leaves her children with a friend, saying she'll be gone overnight. She returns eighteen months later on crutches, with one leg missing, but then begins receiving a series of regular checks in the mail. Although she is mysterious about what happened to her leg, the other characters assume that she allowed a train to run over it and cut it off so that she could collect the insurance money. She doesn't let her lack of a leg interfere with her enjoyment of life, or her enjoyment of men; she is famed for her gentlemen callers—although she never makes love with them—and for the fact that her remaining leg, still shapely, is "stockinged and shod at all times." She lives in a huge, rambling house with many rooms and passageways, takes in boarders—some paying, some not—and spends most of her time high up in the house, watching over the assortment of people in it. These include three boys, all of whom she has named "Dewey."

Everyone in the community admires Eva, despite her nontraditional life. Sula is the one person who does not admire her, however, and when Eva jumps from the second story of the house in order to save Hannah, Sula's mother, who is burning to death, Sula doesn't help either her mother or her grandmother. Later, Sula puts Eva in a nursing home.

Eva is a tough woman, a survivor, who is often brutally honest. Near the end of the book, she is visited by Sula's friend Nel, and reminds Nel that Nel, like Sula, was involved in Chicken Little's death; in the end, she forces Nel to contemplate about her and Sula's likeness.

Eva Peace II

Eva, known as Pearl, is Hannah's sister and Sula's aunt. She marries at fourteen, moves to Flint, Michigan, and writes occasional sad letters to her mother about minor troubles.

Hannah Peace

Hannah is Sula's mother. She married "a laughing man named Rekus" who died when Sula was three; after this, Hannah moves back into Eva Peace's big house, "prepared to take care of it and her mother forever." Like Eva, Hannah loves men, and has a steady stream of lovers, most of whom are married to her friends or neighbors. However, despite her promiscuity, she is leery of trusting anyone or becoming committed to anyone. Hannah is disliked by the "good" women in town, who find her morally reprehensible; by the prostitutes, who resent her for cutting into their business by giving her services away; and also by the "middling women" who have both husbands and affairs, because her lack of passion about her affairs seems strange and alien to them. Hannah is similarly detached from her own daughter, Sula; she loves Sula, but says she doesn't like her.

Ralph Peace

Ralph, known as Plum, is Eva's youngest child, and the one "to whom she hoped to bequeath everything." He goes off to fight in World War I and, like Shadrack, comes home damaged; he has become a heroin addict. When he finally returns to Medallion, his hair is uncombed and uncut, his clothes are dirty, and he is not wearing socks. "But he did have a black bag, a paper sack, and a sweet, sweet smile." He moves back into Eva's house, where he seldom eats or talks to anyone. When Eva realizes that he is an addict, she pours kerosene over him, sets him on fire, and kills him. High on the drug, Plum is unaware of what she's doing.

Sula Peace

Toni Morrison wrote in the *Michigan Quarterly Review*,

> I always thought of Sula as quintessentially black, metaphysically black, if you will, which is not melanin and certainly not unquestioning fidelity to the tribe. She is new world black and new world woman extracting choice from choicelessness, responding intuitively to found things. Improvisational. Daring, disruptive, imaginative, modern, out-of-the-house, outlawed, unpolicing, uncontained and uncontainable. And dangerously female.

Sula, as Morrison notes, is a dark character, not simply because of the color of her skin, but in terms of her soul. She is a strange child, defiant and different from other children. Although this difference seems innate in her, it is exacerbated by two occurrences in her childhood: one when she overhears her mother saying she loves Sula, but doesn't like her, and another when she is inadvertently responsible for the death of a little boy called Chicken Little. As a result of these events, Sula feels unloved and burdened by guilt.

Sula's mother, Hannah, values her independence from others, and Sula follows in her footsteps. The two times that she has a relationship and violates her rule of separateness, she is devastated. She falls in love once, with Ajax, and becomes so obsessed with him that he's frightened away, leaving her miserable.

More long-lasting is Sula's relationship with her best friend, Nel, who is from a very different background and has a very different personality. The two balance each other, and Sula is deeply attached to Nel. After Nel's wedding to a man named Jude, she leaves her hometown of Medallion for ten years. When she comes back, she's changed: she now has a college education and wears expensive clothes. These changes only make the townspeople, who have always regarded her as strange, feel even more alienated from her, to the point where whenever anything bad happens in the town, Sula is blamed.

She also puts her grandmother, Eva, in a

nursing home, leading the town to further reject her. A year later, she is very sick with an unspecified but very painful illness. On her deathbed, she thinks about her alienation from all the people she's known: "The deweys, Tar Baby, the newly married couples, Mr. Buckland Reed, Patsy, Valentine, and the beautiful Hannah Peace. Where were they?" She has lost track of them all, and now she lies alone, "upstairs in Eva's bed with a boarded-up window and an empty pocketbook on the dresser." Even Nel, who has visited her and gotten a painkiller for her, has left and closed the door. Sula thinks about Nel:

> So she will walk on down that road,
> her back so straight in that old green
> coat, the strap of her handbag pushed
> back all the way to the elbow,
> thinking how much I have cost her
> and never remember the days when
> we were two throats and one eye and
> we had no price.

She feels that their old, deep kinship is gone, like her connections to the other people she remembers.

She also thinks of life with a sense of futility: "Nothing was ever different. They were all the same. All of the words and all of the smiles, every tear and every gag just something to do." And in the end, just before she dies, she is comforted by the boarded-up window that Eva jumped out of: "The sealed window soothed her with its sturdy termination, its unassailable finality. It was as though for the first time she was completely alone

—where she had always wanted to be—free of the possibility of distraction."

However, after she dies, the first thing she thinks is, "It didn't even hurt. Wait'll I tell Nel," showing that despite her feeling of alienation, their friendship is deeper than she realized, continuing on past death.

On her deathbed, she thinks about her mother's comments about her, and about Chicken Little's death, and decides that she has lived a meaningless life.

Later in the book, when her mother's dress catches on fire, Sula watches with calm detachment as her mother is fatally burned. Although some of Eva's friends later rationalize her calm watching as the result of being "struck dumb" with shock, Eva "remained convinced that Sula had watched Hannah burn not because she was paralyzed, but because she was interested."

Pearl

See Eva Peace II

Plum

See Ralph Peace

Cecile Sabat

Cecile is Helene Sabat Wright's grandmother.

She takes Helene away from her prostitute mother and raises her in a strict Catholic household.

Rochelle Sabat

Rochelle is Helene's mother. She sees Helene for the first time in sixteen years when Helene's grandmother, Cecile, dies and Helene returns to New Orleans for the funeral. The two look at each other with no recognition or warmth, and similarly, Rochelle is not warm to Nel, her own granddaughter. She is still vibrant and young-looking, and wears a canary-yellow dress and fragrant perfume. Nel is fascinated by her, but Helene is only too eager to get back to Medallion; she has made a break with her past, and she refuses to speak Creole, as Rochelle does, or to teach it to Nel.

Shadrack

Shadrack is shell-shocked from his participation in World War I, and after being released from a veteran's hospital, is arrested by police who assume he's drunk, then released. He drinks to medicate his mental turmoil, and lives in a shack near the river. He is famous in the Bottom as the inventor of "National Suicide Day," which he celebrates every January 3rd, leading a parade through town that most people avoid. Despite this, the holiday becomes part of the town's consciousness, so that people will date events by whether they occurred after or before a particular

Suicide Day.

The only person who ever enters Shadrack's cabin is Sula, who runs there to see if Shadrack has seen her accidentally throw Chicken Little into the river and drown him. Shadrack doesn't give her a chance to ask her question, and simply says "always," which Sula perceives as a threat. However, because she is the only person who has ever visited him, Shadrack views her as his friend for the rest of his life. She has no idea that her life has given a sense of love and meaning to Shadrack. After Sula dies, he loses interest in his invented holiday, "National Suicide Day," and has to force himself to go, but the townspeople, who are depressed from the sudden downward turn of events following Sula's death, eagerly join the parade. The ensuing mob heads toward a half-finished tunnel that is being built mostly by white people, and, filled with hatred for the whites, they begin destroying it. They do so much damage that the tunnel caves in, killing the people inside it, while Shadrack stands on a hill above this scene of mass destruction (and inadvertent mass suicide) ringing a bell.

Tar Baby

Tar Baby is one of the boarders in Eva's house, "a beautiful, slight, quiet man who never spoke above a whisper." Most people think he is halfwhite, but Eva thinks he is totally white, and calls him Tar Baby as a joke. He lives simply, and when he loses his job, he scrounges around for odd jobs, buys liquor, and comes home to drink, but he is no trouble to anyone. Eventually it becomes clear that he simply wants a place to die, privately, but not entirely alone.

Helene Wright

Helene Sabat, born in a brothel in New Orleans to a Creole prostitute, was taken away from her original home as a baby, and raised by her grandmother, who told her to be on guard for any evidence of her mother's "wild blood" and brought her up in a strict Catholic household. Helene marries Wiley Wright, and despite his frequent and long absences, is delighted when she has a daughter, Nel, whom she raises as strictly as her grandmother raised her; however, because there is no Catholic church in Medallion, she joins the most conservative black church instead. Helene is famed in Medallion as an impressive, upstanding woman, a pillar of her church. The only battle she loses is over her name; the townspeople, who refuse to say "Helene," simply call her "Helen."

Nel Wright

An only child, Nel is brought up in a strict, quiet, orderly house, but she longs for excitement, variety, and adventure. She finds them in the company of Sula, her best friend. Although Nel has been brought up in a strict and orderly household— or because of her upbringing there—she hates the "oppressive neatness" of her mother's house and loves "Sula's woolly house," where something is always cooking on the stove, Sula's mother never scolds or tells her what to do, there's a constant chaos of people stopping in, and where one-legged Eva presides, handing out peanuts and telling her dreams.

The two of them are inseparable, each finding something in the other to fill a hole in her own life. Morrison writes that Nel's parents "had succeeded in rubbing down to a dull glow any sparkle or splutter she had." Only with Sula did that quality have free reign, but their friendship was so close, they themselves had difficulty distinguishing one's thoughts from the other's. They are also bound together at a young age by their shared knowledge of exactly how Chicken Little drowned.

Eva grows up to be a traditional, quiet, "good" woman; she has a big wedding, to her mother's delight, has three children, and plans to have a quiet, orderly life. This plan is destroyed when she finds her husband and Sula having an affair.

When Sula is dying, Nel visits her for the first time in three years, since Sula's affair with Jude. They are uneasy with each other but pick up the relationship where it left off. Nel tells Sula she should be with someone who can take care of her, but Sula refuses. Nel is also offended by Sula's arrogant talk about how she doesn't need any man, never would have worked for anyone else, and doesn't need anyone now. She asks Sula why she had an affair with Jude, and Sula says it was just because Jude filled up a space in her life; Nel is hurt that she, as Sula's friend, didn't count to fill up any space. She can't get a straight answer from Sula about what their friendship meant to Sula, and realizes, "She can't give a sensible answer because she didn't know." The last thing Sula asks her is, "About who was good. How did you know it was you?" calling into question her identity as a "good" girl and a "good" woman. After Sula dies, however, the first thing Sula thinks is "Wait'll I tell Nel," showing that their friendship has endured past these difficulties, past death.

Themes

Poverty and Hopelessness

Throughout the novel, the lives of the characters are shaped by poverty, as they have little or no money, unlike many of their white counterparts in the town. Although no one in the book is rich, the people of the Bottom are exceptionally poor. Eva has money only because she sacrificed her leg; others must make do as they can, with menial jobs or no jobs, because work for African Americans is limited by the racism of those who could hire them. When characters have dreams, like Jude, who dreams of doing a man's work on the road crew instead of spending a menial day as a waiter, they are crushed.

Existence in the Bottom is precarious at best, and is easily disrupted. Near the end of the book, people's hopes are raised by rumors that the new tunnel construction would use African-American laborers, and by the fact that an old people's home that was being renovated would be open to African Americans. However, these hopes are forgotten when a freezing rain kills all the late crops, kills chickens, splits jugs of cider, and makes the "thin houses and thinner clothes" of the Bottom people seem even thinner. Housebound, they make do with what they have, since deliveries have stopped and the good food is all being saved for white customers anyway. Thanksgiving that year is a meal of "tiny tough birds, heavy pork cakes, and pithy sweet potatoes." By spring all the children are sick and the adults are suffering from a variety of ailments.

All this suffering and malaise is accompanied by "a falling away, a dislocation." Mothers slap their children and resent the old people they have to take care of, wives and husbands become alienated from each other, and people begin bickering about small things. Christmas that year is a misery because of the sickness, lack of good food, and absence of money for gifts. The only gifts they can get are bags of rock candy and old clothes, given away by white people.

This feeling of doom and hopelessness leads almost everyone in town to participate in that year's celebration of National Suicide Day, with a feeling of reckless abandon at the idea of "looking at death in the sunshine and being unafraid," as well as the feeling of "this respite from anxiety, from dignity, from gravity, from the weight of the very adult pain that had undergirded them all those years before … as though there really was hope." This is the same hope that has kept them laboring in white men's beanfields in hopes of bettering themselves, fighting in other people's wars, kept them solicitous of white people's children, "kept them convinced that some magic 'government' was going to lift them up, out and away from that dirt, those beans, those wars." In other words, it's a futile and misguided hope.

Caught up in the energy of the moment, seeking release, the crowd of people pours on down the New River Road toward the tunnel, where they see "the place where their hope had lain since 1927. There was the promise: leaf-dead. The teeth unrepaired, the coal credit cut off, the chest pains unattended, the school shoes unbought, the rush-stuffed mattresses … the slurred remarks and the staggering childish malevolence of their employers." They try to destroy the tunnel, but in their desire to destroy it, they enter it and ultimately destroy themselves when the tunnel collapses under their attack.

Topics for Further Study

- Research the Jim Crow laws and describe how they affected every area of life for African Americans.

- Find out about the Civil Rights movements of the 1960s and discuss their effectiveness. What issues do you think still need to be addressed to ensure equality among different groups of people?

- Research the contributions of African-American soldiers in World War I or World War II. Choose a particular soldier and write about his life before, during, and after the war.

- How do you feel racism affects you? Write an essay about your experiences.

- In the book, relationships between mothers and daughters are difficult and painful. Do you think this is the case for most mothers and daughters? Why or why not?

- Choose a character from the book and write a story about his or her experiences during a period that is not covered in the book. For example, write about Sula's life during her ten years away from Medallion, or Shadrack's life during the war.

Good and Evil

A major theme running through the book is good versus evil, and the fact that what people think is evil may be good, and vice versa. Shadrack, who appears in the first chapter, is considered dangerous and evil by the townspeople, and when he says "Always" to Sula, she takes it as a threat. However, he is not evil, he is simply shell-shocked and misunderstood; throughout the book, he never harms anyone. Sula is also considered evil, especially in the second half of the book, and Nel is considered good, but by the end of the book, Nel realizes that she has evil thoughts and has done evil things, while Sula has inspired the most good acts that the town has ever seen.

Eva, Sula's grandmother, is considered good, respectable, and a pillar of the community, but actually has a darker side. Her ruthlessness is hinted at by the rumor that she arranged to have own her leg cut off, a scene that is reflected by Sula when she cuts off the tip of her own finger to frighten off some harassing white boys. If she's able to do that to herself, she tells them, they should just think about what she'd be able to do to them. Sula's minor act of self-mutilation pales in comparison with Eva's, and the unspoken question the book asks is, "If she's able to do that to herself, what would she be willing to do to someone else?" The answer is, "Anything and everything," including killing her own son by pouring kerosene over him and setting him on fire while he's in a drug-induced haze.

Racism

The novel explores the relationship between the races, which is marred by racism and bigotry. In the opening scene, the founding of the Bottom is described; according to local legend, the area became the property of African Americans when a white man deceived a slave into thinking the high, dry, and eroded land was good for farming because it was the "bottom" of heaven. When Chicken Little is drowned, his body is found by a white man, who has no compassion for the dead child or his family, but who is merely annoyed at having to deal with the mess. On the train south, Helene and Nel experience degrading treatment at the hands of the white conductor and the white-run train system, which does not provide restrooms for African Americans. When Jude tries to get a job with the road-building crew, he is denied one, although the company hires scrawny whites who obviously can't do as good a job as he can; he can only get a job as a waiter, which he feels is servile and degrading. When Sula returns to town after a ten-year absence, her erratic behavior causes the townspeople to spread rumors about her causing all of their misfortunes, and the most damning rumor about her is that she willingly sleeps with white men.

Mothers and Daughters

Throughout the book, the many mother-daughter pairs have strained, unhappy relationships, and the lack of love a mother has for her daughter is passed on through the generations. In Nel's family, her grandmother, Cecile, disapproved of Rochelle, her prostitute daughter, and took Helene, Rochelle's daughter, away from Rochelle. Rochelle and Helene don't even know each other and are as alienated as

Rochelle was from her mother. Nel, Helene's daughter, who is similarly alienated from Nel, feels oppressed by her mother's strictness and propriety, and feels stifled in her quiet, orderly house.

Eva, Hannah's mother, is an outwardly up-standing and secretly ruthless woman, and it's clear that her daughter, Hannah, didn't feel loved by her. At one point, she even asks Eva if she loved her children, a question that makes Eva angry. Hannah is also ambivalent about her daughter, Sula; Sula overhears her telling some friends that although she loves Sula, she doesn't like her, a comment that deeply wounds Sula. Because of this, Sula grows up feeling unloved and left out.

Point of View

The novel is told from the point of view of a wise, omniscient narrator, who sees into all the characters' hearts and minds with tolerance and acceptance. The use of such a narrator is interesting; the characters are all given equal time, and no one, even Sula—for whom the book is named—is more major than anyone else. In addition, the use of varied points of view allows the reader to see all the sides of any event and understand the complexity of what really happened. In the book, horrendous events are depicted, but the narrator avoids making judgments about them; they are simply presented, and the reader sees various characters respond to them and is allowed to come to an independent determination of what these things mean and whether they are good or evil.

Realistic Dialogue

The author frequently uses dialect speech, bringing the characters to life and letting the reader hear them talk, in a very natural way. For example, in the following dialogue between Eva and Hannah, Hannah has just asked Eva if she loved her children and played with them when they were little, and Eva deflects the question by telling her about the hard times she went through:

"I'm talkin' 'bout 18 and 95 when I set in that house five days with you and Pearl and Plum and three beets, you snake-eyed ungrateful hussy. What would I look like leapin' 'round that little old room playin' with youngins with three beets to my name?"

"I know 'bout them beets, Mamma. You told us that a million times."

"Yeah? Well? Don't that count? Ain't that love? You want me to tinkle you under the jaw and forget 'bout them sores in your mouth?"

By using dialect speech, Morrison allows us to hear the characters as real people, and shows their social class, education, and attitudes without having to explicitly discuss these aspects. We know from their talk that the characters are African American, poor, and most likely rural. They express themselves directly, with no social posturing or pretension; their speech is vigorous and active, full of energy and passion.

Although white people rarely appear in the novel, when they do, they also speak in dialect. In the case of the conductor on the train to the south, it's southern: he asks Helene, "What was you doin' back in there? What was you doin' in that coach yonder?" When she tells him she made a mistake and got in the white car by accident, he says, "We don't 'low no mistakes on this train. Now git your butt on in there." His dialect talk makes him seem uneducated and harsh at the same time that it underlines his similarity to the African Americans he despises, since the things he says, and the way he says them, could easily have been said by anyone in the Bottom in the same way. This similarity provides a subtle commentary on the misguided nature of racism, which erects artificial boundaries between people. He thinks he's "better" than the people in the "colored" car, but he is not as different from them as he'd like to believe.

Use of a Prologue

Sula, like many other novels, but unlike any of Morrison's other works, has a prologue that describes the Bottom and its origin, and makes the reader aware that this is a book about African-American people, set in an African-American settlement. In a discussion about the book in the *Michigan Quarterly Review*, Morrison noted that her original beginning simply began, "Except for World War II nothing ever interfered with National Suicide Day." After getting some feedback about the book from others, she realized that this was too sudden a beginning, and that it didn't make clear to the reader where the book was set or what was going on. She thought of the prologue as a "safe, welcoming lobby," and believed it was necessary to make readers comfortable in her African-American world before they could move on with the story. She said that she would not need this "lobby" now, and indeed, none of her other books have this "lobby"; they refuse, she said, "to cater to the diminished expectations of the reader or his or her alarm heightened by the emotional luggage one carries into the black-topic text." She also said, "I despise much of this beginning," and noted that her other books "refuse the 'presentation'; refuse the seductive safe harbor; the line of demarcation between … them and us."

Historical Context

The events in *Sula* span much of the twentieth century, during a time of great changes in civil rights for African Americans and other minority groups.

African Americans in World War I

When the events of the book open, in 1919, veterans like Shadrack and Plum are returning from service overseas. Like Shadrack and Plum, many of them were emotionally and physically scarred from the experience of war, but African-American veterans did not receive as much respect for their service as their white counterparts. In the book, Shadrack is discharged from the hospital because there's no more room, and when he hits the streets, whites assume he's drunk, and he's arrested and taken to jail. All he has to show for his service is "$217 in cash, a full suit of clothes and copies of very official-looking papers."

During the war, more than 350,000 African-American soldiers served in segregated units. When they returned, many began working for civil rights, reasoning that if they were considered good enough to fight and risk their lives for their country, they should be given full participation in society. Both African Americans and whites joined the newly formed NAACP to fight discrimination and segregation, but it would be many years before segregation laws would be overturned.

African Americans had only recently been given the right to vote in the United States. Although they had supposedly held this right for much longer, various loopholes in the law ensured that few did. One law stated that an African-American man could vote only if his grandfather had. Poll taxes, literacy tests, voting fraud, violence against those who voted, and intimidation also kept people away from the ballot box. The NAACP fought successfully against the "grandfather clause," and it was overturned in 1915, but some of the other blocks to voting remained for many years.

The Great Depression

In 1929, the stock market crashed, leading to widespread depression and deep poverty. Skilled and unskilled, African-American and white, few people escaped the suffering involved. When Franklin Delano Roosevelt was elected in 1932, he presented "New Deal" programs that would help housing, agriculture, and economic interests. Although African Americans had fewer opportunities than whites to benefit from the New Deal programs, they did participate in some of them.

Segregation

Through laws known as "Jim Crow" laws, Southern states were forcefully segregated, with separate facilities for travel, overnight lodging, eating, drinking, school, church, housing, and other services for African Americans and whites. These facilities were separate, and many times not equal; those for African Americans were frequently substandard or nonexistent. If an African American failed to obey the segregation laws, he or she could be arrested and imprisoned.

World War II and the Civil Rights Movement

Many African Americans served in World War II, and like those who served in World War I, returned home and were outraged that they could serve their country but yet not have equal rights in it. The civil rights movement grew with protests, nonviolent resistance, boycotts, and rallies, which received increasing attention in the national media. In addition, activists challenged the segregation laws in court. In 1948, President Harry Truman eliminated segregation in the United States armed forces. Through other battles, segregation in other areas of life, such as on buses and in schools, was attacked and outlawed, although racist incidents continued to cause trouble for African Americans, and other areas of life were not yet integrated.

Compare & Contrast

- **1920s:** More than 350,000 African-American soldiers, who serve in segregated units, return home from World War I.

Today: The United States armed forces include large numbers of African Americans, who serve in every capacity and are no longer segregated; some African Americans, such as General Colin Powell, U.S. Secretary of State during the administration of George W. Bush, achieve the highest rank.

- **1920s:** Overall, the unemployment rate is about 5.2%, but this figure is much higher for African Americans because of prejudice against them.

  Today: Unemployment ranges between 5 and 6 percent and African Americans are integrated into all sectors of society, thought they still experience a higher level of unemployment than whites.

- **1920s:** "Jim Crow" laws, which were implemented in the late nineteenth century, segregate the South, mandating separate spheres of existence for African Americans and whites. Restaurants, stores, buses, hotels, transportation, housing, and other areas of life are rigidly separated, and African Americans who cross the barriers can be arrested and imprisoned.

Today: The widespread and growing civil rights movement brings increasing attention to the problems caused by discrimination and segregation. Although old laws restricting African Americans from voting and full participation in society were finally overturned in the 1960s, racism, bigotry, and other prejudices still exist and act to restrict full participation for many people.

In 1963, more than 200,000 people joined the March on Washington, calling national attention to the problems of segregation and discrimination. Dr. Martin Luther King, Jr. delivered his famed "I Have a Dream" speech, calling for racial equality.

In 1965, the Voting Rights Act finally outlawed the use of literacy tests and other methods to exclude African Americans from voting. Before this law, only about twenty-three percent of African Americans were registered to vote, but after it, registration jumped to sixty-one percent.

The Civil Rights Act of 1968, known as the Fair Housing Act, more forcefully ensured that African Americans were legally entitled to all the rights that went with full citizenship in the United States.

Critical Overview

As Paul Gray noted in *Time*, some reviewers have found Morrison's work "overly deterministic, her characters pawns in the service of their creator's designs." He quoted essayist Stanley Crouch, who commented that Morrison was "immensely talented. I just think she needs a new subject matter, the world she lives in, not this world of endless black victims." However, Gray also noted: "For every pan, Morrison has received a surfeit of paeans: for her lyricism, for her ability to turn the mundane into the magical."

In the *New York Times Book Review*, Sara Blackburn commented that *Sula* was "a more precise yet somehow icy version of [Morrison's first novel] *The Bluest Eye*," and that "it refuses to invade our present in the way we want it to and stays, instead, confined to its time and place." Although, as Blackburn noted, Morrison's dialogue is "so compressed and lifelike that it sizzles" and her characterization is so skillful that the people in the book "seem almost mythologically strong and familiar," somehow "we can't imagine their surviving outside the tiny community where they carry on their separate lives." Because of this, she wrote, the novel's "longrange impact doesn't sustain the quality of its first reading." Blackburn also commented that Morrison was too talented to continue writing about "the black side of provincial American life" and that if she wanted to maintain a "large and serious audience," she would have to address a "riskier contemporary reality."

In addition, interestingly, Blackburn confessed that she, like other reviewers, might have given Morrison's first novel, *The Bluest Eye*, more attention than it might have deserved. "Socially conscious readers—including myself—were so pleased to see a new writer of Morrison's obvious talent that we tended to celebrate the book and ignore its flaws." Presumably, she did not do this for *Sula*.

In the *Journal of Black Studies;* Marie Nigro wrote that the book is "an unforgettable story of the friendship of two African-American woman and ... graciously allowed us to enter the community of the Bottom." By writing the book, Morrison "has given us an understanding of social, psychological, and sociological issues that might have been evident only to African Americans."

Jane S. Bakerman, in *American Literature*, wrote that "Morrison has undertaken a difficult task in *Sula*. Unquestionably, she has succeeded." She also praised Morrison's use of the tale of Sula and Nel's maturation as a core for the many other stories in the book, and said that as the main unifying device of the novel, "It achieves its own unity, again, through the clever manipulation of the themes of sex, race, and love."

In *Black Women Writers: A Critical Evaluation*, Darwin T. Turner praised Morrison's "verbal descriptions that carry the reader deep into the soul of the character.... Equally effective, however, is her art of narrating action in a lean prose that uses adjectives cautiously while creating memorable vivid images."

Jonathan Yardley, in the *Washington Post Book World*, noted that a chief distinction of the novel is "the quality of Toni Morrison's prose ... [The book's] real strength lies in Morrison's writing, which at times has the resonance of poetry and is precise, vivid and controlled throughout."

In the *Harvard Advocate*, Faith Davis wrote that a "beautiful and haunting atmosphere emerges out of the wreck of these folks' lives, a quality that is absolutely convincing and absolutely precise."

The novel was nominated for a National Book Award in 1974, but did not win.

What Do I Read Next?

- Morrison's *Beloved* (1987), written

in an episodic, experimental style, examines the heritage of slavery.

- Morrison's first novel, *The Bluest Eye* (1970), stars Pecola, who prays each night for blue eyes, hoping that if she gets them she will finally be noticed and loved.

- Morrison's *Jazz* (1992) tells the story of a triangle of passion, jealousy, murder, and redemption.

- In *Song of Solomon* (1977), Morrison tells the story of Macon Dead, an upper-middle-class African-American entrepreneur who tries to isolate his family from other African Americans in the neighborhood, and how this affects his son.

- *Tar Baby* (1981), by Morrison, describes a love affair between an African-American model and a white man.

- In *Playing in the Dark: Whiteness and the Literary Imagination* (1992), Morrison discusses the significance of African Americans in American literature.

- Alice Walker's *The Temple of My Familiar* (1989) intertwines the lives of many people from the United States, England, and Africa, and provides perspectives on the colonial African experience as well as the experiences of African Americans.

- In *The Color Purple* (1982), Alice Walker describes an abused woman's struggle for empowerment.

Sources

Bakerman, Jane S., Review of *Sula*, in *American Literature*, March 1980, pp. 87-100.

Blackburn, Sara, "You Still Can't Go Home Again," in *New York Times Book Review*, December 30, 1973.

Davis, Faith, Review of *Sula*, in *Harvard Advocate*, Vol. 107, No. 4, 1974.

Gray, Paul, "Paradise Found," in *Time*, January 19, 1998.

Morrison, Toni, "The Salon Interview: Toni Morrison," in Salon, http://www.salon.com/ (July 23, 2001).

—————, "Unspeakable Things Spoken: The Afro-American Presence in American Literature," in *Michigan Quarterly Review*, Vol. 28, Winter 1989, pp. 1-34.

—————, *Voices from the Gaps: Women Writers of Color*, http://voices.cla.umn.edu/authors/ToniMorrison.htm (July 23, 2001).

Nigro, Marie, "In Search of Self: Frustration and Denial in Toni Morrison's *Sula*," in *Journal of Black Studies*, Vol. 28, No. 6, July 1998, p. 724.

O'Brien, Maureen, "Novelist Toni Morrison Wins Nobel Prize for Literature," in *Publishers Weekly*, October 11, 1993, p. 7.

Turner, Darwin T., *Black Women Writers (1950–1980): A Critical Evaluation*, edited by Mari Evans, Doubleday, 1984.

Yardley, Jonathan, Review of *Sula*, in *Washington Post Book World*," February 3, 1974.

For Further Reading

Angelo, Bonnie, "The Pain of Being Black," in *Time*, May 22, 1989.

> In this interview, Morrison discusses racism in society and in her novels.

Basu, Biman, "The Black Voice and the Language of the Text: Toni Morrison's *Sula*," in *College Literature*, October 1996, p. 88.

> This article discusses Morrison's use of African-American vernacular in the novel.

Bloom, Harold, ed., *Toni Morrison's "Sula*," Modern Critical Interpretations series, Chelsea House, 1999.

> This is a compendium of critical essays on *Sula*.

Carabi, Angels, "Toni Morrison," in *Belles Lettres: A Review of Books by Women*, Spring 1995, p. 40.

> In this interview, Morrison discusses her novel, *Jazz*, and race in American society during the middle of the twentieth century.

Grewal, Gurleen, *Circles of Sorrow, Lives of Struggle: The Novels of Toni Morrison*, Louisiana State University Press, 1998.

> This critical text examines

Morrison's novels and the African-American experience.

Rice, Herbert William, ed., *Toni Morrison: A Rhetorical Reading*, Peter Lang Publishers, 1996.

This collection of critical works on Morrison examines her work and its place in American literature.

Ryan, Katy, "Revolutionary Suicide in Toni Morrison's Fiction," in *African American Review*, Fall 2000.

This scholarly article discusses the theme of suicide in Morrison's works.

Samuels, Wilfred D., and Clenora Hudson-Weems, *Toni Morrison*, Twayne Publishers, 1990.

This critical volume describes Morrison's life and work.

Printed in the USA
CPSIA information can be obtained
at www.ICGtesting.com
LVHW050002131023
760951LV00004B/528

9 781375 388979